TABLE OF CONTENTS

6	The Big Picture
18	From Vine To Bottle
30	The Finished Product
36	Color, Smell & Taste
46	Putting It All Together

GREETINGS!

I am The Wine Doctor, and I created a fun, easy-to-read educational blog about wine which can be found at *www.thewinemd.com*. Please check it out if you haven't already, and subscribe so you always know when I have posted new content.

As I note in the opening page to my website, wine is the culmination of love, hard work, science and luck. It has a life of its own. It changes and evolves…every year. Because it is constantly changing, that means there is always something new to learn, something new to experience. It is part of what keeps you coming back!

To help you learn and grow your wine confidence, I created a page on the site called **Wine 101**. It covers some basics that will help you better understand and appreciate what is in your glass.

I thought it might be helpful to enrich my Wine 101 content and create a handy, stand-alone reference book. The result is what you are now holding in your hand.

So, without any further introduction, let's get started!

THE BIG PICTURE

OLD WORLD VS NEW WORLD:
Wait, what if I'm not good at geography?

Not to worry, this is actually pretty easy to understand. Old World wines are from regions where winemaking originated. Think France, Italy, Spain, etc. New World wines come from places where winemaking and grapes "migrated". Think United States, Australia, South Africa, South America, etc.

Broadly, Old World wines are often characterized as being lighter and less fruity than their new world counter-parts. Old World wines are often higher in acidity as well. Winemaking tradition as well as soil & climate (see "Terroir" later) are major contributors to differences between Old and New World wines.

More on all this wine characteristics stuff later.

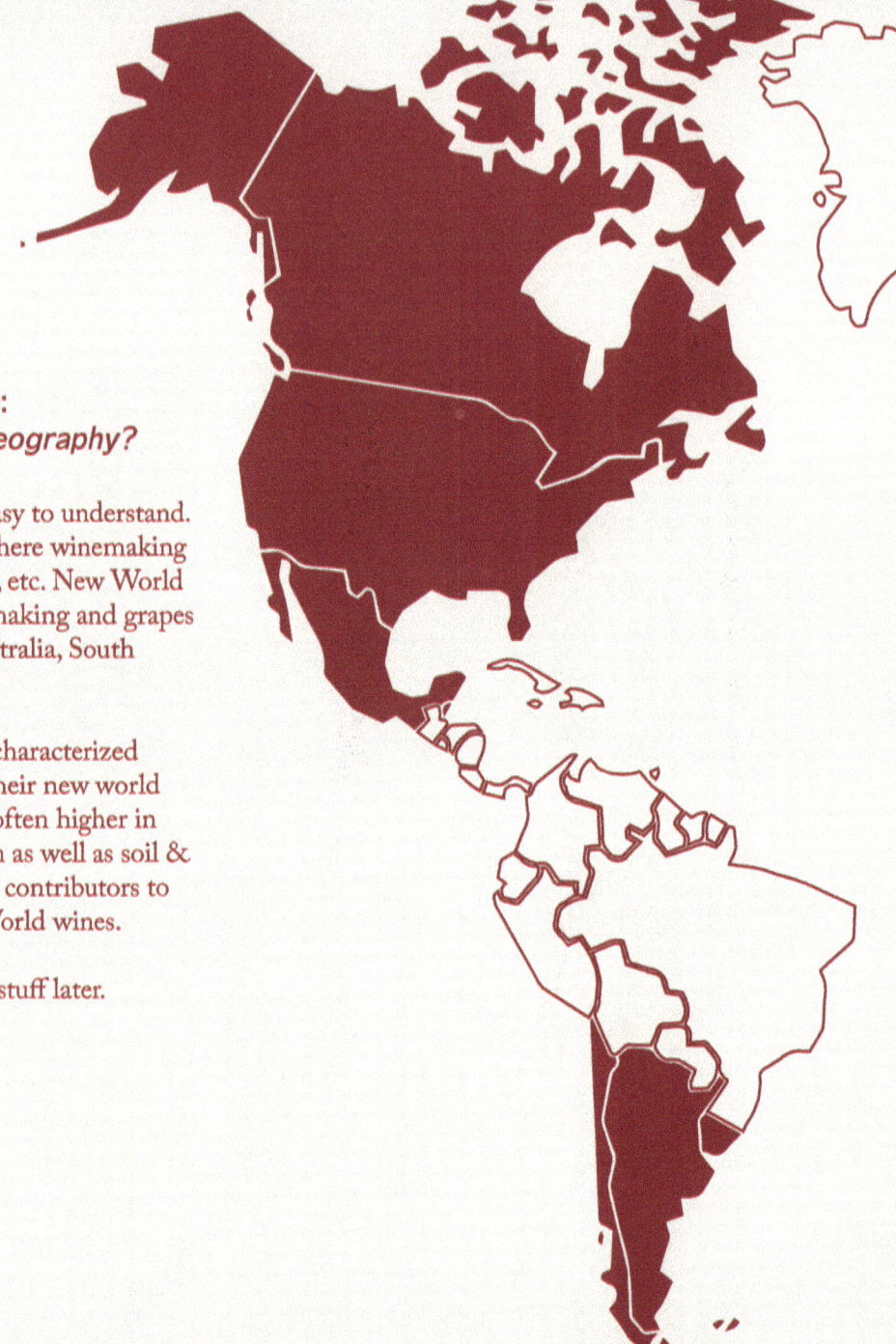

VARIETAL:
a fancy word for "grape"

When you hear or see the word varietal, it is referring to a single grape variety, such as Chardonnay, Merlot, Cabernet Sauvignon, etc. A single-varietal wine will be made wholly, or, depending on the region, mostly with that particular grape variety. In the US, that percentage is usually 75%. Outside the US, that percentage is higher, often 85%. We will revisit this topic when talking about labels.

DRY VS SWEET

The degree of sweetness found in wine is a function of something called "residual sugar", which is the unfermented sugars from the grape which remain in the wine after fermentation. Without getting too technical, most still wines we consume are categorized as either "Dry", "off-Dry" or "Sweet". Sparkling wines will add a small amount of a concentrated grape "must" or "sugar" toward the end of the winemaking process. You will see terms describing the relative sweetness of sparkling wine (from dry to sweet) like "Extra Brut", "Brut", "Extra Dry", "Dry", to "Demi-Sec".

TO BLEND OR NOT TO BLEND?

If a wine does not contain a high enough percentage to be designated single-varietal, then it is simply referred to as a blend. There are more blends out there than you think, and in some wine making regions of the world, blending two or more grape varietals is standard practice. By blending, the winemaker can take advantage of different grape characteristics to create a unique finished product. Perhaps nowhere else is blending so prominent and established than in the Bordeaux region of France.

Bordeaux – One of the classic wine producing regions of France. Home to some of the world's great red wines, winemakers in Bordeaux have been making wines which are a blend of two or more grapes for hundreds of years. These blends are usually Cabernet Sauvignon-based, or Merlot-based. Other varietals you will find playing supporting roles include Cabernet Franc, Malbec and Petit Verdot.

Blends can be found in many other great wine producing regions of the world. In the Rhone Valley of France, you will find some combination of Grenache, Syrah and Mourvedre (so-called "GSM" blends), but other varietals can be used as well. In Italy, "Super Tuscan" blends usually feature some combination of Sangiovese with other varietals such as Merlot and Cabernet Sauvignon. Blending is also popular in Spain, Australia and the United States.

VINTAGE

Very simply, vintage means the year in which the grapes were harvested. As we shall see, quite a lot of time can elapse between the harvesting of the grapes, the bottling of the wine, and the ultimate release to the public of that "vintage".

Vintage becomes a key reference point when evaluating the general quality of wine produced in a particular region. How good the wines are from that region are a function of many inputs, but one of the biggest contributors year in and year out is of course the weather!

Sunshine, rain and temperature all play a role in the ultimate quality of the harvest. Too much or too little of any of them and the grapes will not ripen properly. The closer you get to harvest time, the greater the risk of bad weather impacting quality of the grapes, so timing is crucial.

Vintage matters more in areas that have less predictable climates. Conversely, some regions such as Argentina, Australia, California, and parts of Italy and Spain tend to have more consistent growing conditions, and therefore have the potential to produce more consistent quality wines each year.

For people who are serious about collecting fine wine, vintage REALLY matters. If it was a good vintage, many red wines will only get better with age.

If a wine is made from a blend of multiple harvests (years), then it is considered "non-vintage". You are most likely to see this with Champagne, which may carry the letters "N.V." on the label.

TERROIR:
It's more than just soil...

No, I didn't say "terror". Terroir is a French term ("tair-WAH") which refers to the total environment that influences the grapes: soil; climate and topography or terrain. Ultimately, the taste of the wine can bear a "signature" of its terroir. Let's explore these just a little further to make sure we understand how they impact the finished product you are enjoying..

Soil – there are countless variations of soil, mineral and rock deposits in vineyards around the world. Basic soil types are clay-based, sand-based, silt-based or loam-based. Each have different characteristics when it comes to how water and heat are retained. Within these, you can find a variety of mineral deposits such as limestone, gravel, slate or granite. Each can influence how the vines grow and can subtly impart different flavors to the wine.

Climate – Wine regions can be classified as either "cool climate" or "warm climate". Sugar levels and acidity, which we will discuss later, are directly impacted by climate. Warmer climates = higher sugar levels, and cooler climates generally = lower sugar levels and higher acidity.

Terrain – This is a complex component. Terrain encompasses things like altitude, mountains & valleys, vineyard position relative to sun & wind, proximity to water, etc. Terrain can contribute to certain conditions which can be characterized as a "micro-climate".

FROM VINE TO BOTTLE

WHAT'S IN A LABEL?

Deciphering all of the words you find on a wine label can be challenging if not downright intimidating. Not only do you need to understand what the words mean, you often have to read them in a foreign language!

Without going overboard on all the rules and traditions associated with how wines are labeled, there are a few things to remember which will help you better understand what is in the bottle you are looking at, and where it came from. It may be helpful to break this into the two basic categories we just identified - **New World** and **Old World**.

MIS EN BOUTEILLE AU CHÂTEAU

CHATEAU LAFITE ROTHSCHILD
1988
PAUILLAC
APPELLATION PAUILLAC CONTRÔLÉE

NEW WORLD

New World wines are a little easier to understand (assuming you speak English). The key things to look for here are the following:

Producer – This will be the most prominent part of the label, generally at the top in the largest type. This is who made the wine. Usually (but not always) this is the winery/vineyard. However, it doesn't necessarily mean that the Producer made the wine from its own grapes. A winemaker can purchase grapes from one or more independent growers. Up and coming winemakers who don't have the resources to buy their own land and winery can purchase grapes from independent growers and have the wine made (under their direct supervision) at a third-party facility.

Varietal – The next most prominent word on the label is the grape that was used to make the wine (Pinot Noir, Chardonnay, etc.). In the US, if a particular varietal is specified on the front of the label, then at least 75% of the wine must come from that grape.

Viticultural Area – Often abbreviated as "AVA" (American Viticultural Area), these are official designations with specific geographic boundaries and features. In the US, AVAs help you know where the grapes came from that were used to make the wine. To use the AVA name on the label, 85% or more of the grapes must come from that specific geography.

Sometimes, you will just see a broader geographic reference, such as Napa or Sonoma. More often, you will see the name of a smaller, more distinct AVA. For example, in Northern California, more famous AVAs include names such as Russian River Valley, Howell Mountain, Rutherford, Stags Leap District, Dy Creek Valley, and many more.

In the Central Coast, you may see names such as Paso Robles, Edna Valley, Santa Lucia Highlands, to name a few. In the Central Valley, Lodi is a popular AVA.

Vineyard – Sometimes, the winemaker may also list a specific vineyard, a so-called "single vineyard designation". This can be helpful if that plot of land is famous for producing grapes that become top quality wines, year-in and year-out. This does not necessarily mean the Producer owns that vineyard (although he/she certainly can); it highlights a unique and special place where the grapes were grown and sourced.

Estate – When you see the words "Estate Bottled" on the label, it means that 100% of the grapes in your wine were grown, processed and bottled at the same location.

Salta is the region in Argentina where these Malbec grapes are grown

Straightforwward New World label: Producer's name; geography and grape all plainly spelled-out. How easy!

Grand Reserve is a term used by the winemaker to designate their highest quality grapes from this vintage

Doesn't get any easier than this: no guessing what kind of wine this is and where it came from!

OLD WORLD

Old World wine labels can be tough. Besides the language challenges, the rules and designations found on the label vary by country. Here are some basics that might help you as you stand in front of the (French/Italian/Spanish) section of the wine store and your eyes are glazing over:

Region – Regional labeling is common in many European countries. The region is usually prominently located on the label. In these countries, they expect that you know the kind of grape or grapes that are used to make wine in that region!

> For example, the Bordeaux region in France makes wines predominantly from Cabernet Sauvignon and Merlot, but you won't see that on the front of the bottle. Depending on the winemaker, you may get that information in smaller type on the back label.

> Other examples: France is also known for wines such as Sancerre (made from Sauvignon Blanc); Chablis (not a grape- the grape is Chardonnay!); and Burgundy (red Burgundy is made from Pinot Noir and white Burgundy is made from Chardonnay). In Italy, Chianti (also not a grape, it is a region in Tuscany) is made from Sangiovese and Barolo (a region of Piedmont) uses the Nebbiolo grape. In Spain, the famed Rioja region makes great red wine from the Tempranillo grape.

> Easy, right?

The name of the winery: Cascina Adelaide

With this Italian wine, "Barolo" has two meanings: the type of wine as well as the place where it comes from

The quality control designation: "DOCG", highest in Italy

The name of the wine. In this case "Fossati" is the specific vineyard where the grapes are grown

Classic Old World Label: Nowhere does it tell you what Grapes are used to make this wine. You are expected to know that Barolo is made with Nebbiolo grapes!

Often you will see information in the local language. Here, they are telling you the attitude and geographic exposure of the vines

The name of the owner

Required on all bottles: alcohol content ("ABV")

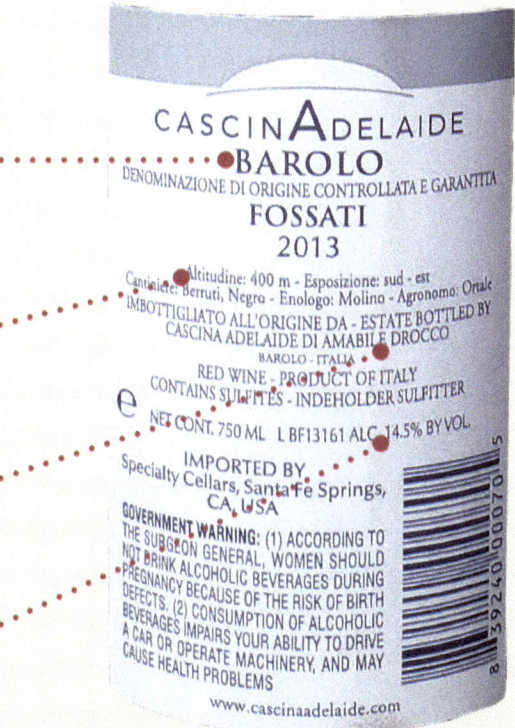

Quality – This is another challenge. Remember our California example with the AVA designation? In the Old World, they can have a similar system, but it really goes beyond geography to focus on the grapes that are permitted to be used, how they are planted and the winemaking process itself. You will find this either on the label (front or back), or sometimes in a band around the neck of the bottle.

Some examples, by country, in order of classification from higher to lower quality:

France: AOC ("Appelation d'Origine Controlee", there are over 300 of them in France); IGP or Vin de Pays (essentially everyday French wine); Vin de France.

Italy: DOCG ("Denominazione di Origine Controllata e Garantita", there are over 70 of these); DOC; IGP/IGT.

Spain: DOP ("Denominacion de Origen Protegida"). Within DOP there are 3 sub-classifications you will find (in order): VP; DOCa/DOQ; DO. After that comes IGP.

Aging – In Italy and especially Spain, you will also see words on the label which conform to aging classifications, for example:

Spain: "Reserva" means a red that has 36 months of aging, with at least 12 in the barrel; "Crianza" means a red with 24 months of aging, with 6 months to a year in barrel.

Italy: "Riserva" varies by region, but generally a year or longer.

The name of the estate where the wine was made

The name of this particular wine: "Maclura" is a kind of fruit tree found on Pegau's land

The region in France where this wine comes from: the Cotes-du-Rhone

Bottled by the producer Laurence Feraud, owner of Chateau Pegau

"Cuvee" translates loosely to "blend"

Great information here: telling us exactly what grapes are used to make the wine. Old World doesnt always give us this!

OAK:
Can I get splinters from wine?

When I say "oak", I am referring to the wooden barrels used to age wine. They can sometimes be used in the fermentation process as well. The wood of choice is oak, which can come from either America or Europe. Each are somewhat different, and can impart different flavor profiles. Oak is used with both red and some white wines

So what does oak do for wine? There are two principal roles oak plays in the process of making wine:

The SLOW penetration of oxygen. The porous nature of the barrel allows oxygen to enter the wine, but not at levels that would threaten the quality of the wine. In fact, at these levels, it actually improves the wine. The effect is to soften the wine's tannins, making it smoother, less astringent. This is oak's textural contribution to wine.

The addition of flavor compounds. Commonly discernable qualities are vanilla, spice, and smoke. When wine comes into contact with oak, particularly new oak, flavor compounds are transferred from the wood to the wine, giving it certain characteristic aromas and flavors. For example, American Chardonnay often has an oaky, creamy, sometimes buttery or vanilla taste. These qualities are brought forward by the winemaker's use of oak, particularly new oak.

The choice of new oak vs used oak will help determine how much flavor contribution will occur in the ageing process. New oak has a more pronounced flavor influence, while older oak may not impart much in the way of flavor, but can still play a role in the permeation of oxygen.

Depending on the varietal and the wine maker's objectives, the wine can age in oak from less than a year for certain whites, to two or more years for certain reds.

Oak barrels are an expensive component of the wine making process. A new barrel can cost around $1,000, and after 3 to 5 years, their useful life is up and they must be replaced.

"So THAT'S why my wine costs so much…" Well, yes, that's one reason..

THE FINISHED PRODUCT

CORK VS SCREW CAPS:
Does screw cap = inferior or cheap?

The short answer is No.

Cork has been used to seal wine bottles for hundreds of years. Most cork comes from a certain kind of tree, most commonly grown in Portugal. It takes months to harvest, dry, prepare and shape the material to where it has the proper elasticity. A good cork allows just the right amount of oxygen to enter the bottle, promoting slow, complex chemical changes inside the bottle so the wine ages gracefully.

Some wine producing regions have embraced screw caps and use them extensively- New Zealand is a good example. It by no means implies a lesser quality product, and in fact some really excellent Sauvignon Blancs come in screw cap bottles from New Zealand.

Nevertheless, there is something to be said for the ritual of inserting the corkscrew into the cork and removing it with one smooth pull that culminates in that satisfying "pop" when it comes out of the bottle. However, given what we just said about the benefit of very gradual oxygen penetration of the cork to help an age-worthy wine achieve its full potential, you probably would not want a big, tannic red built for the long haul to have a screw cap.

AIR:
Friend or foe?

The answer is…YES! As we just learned about Oak, and will discuss later in Tasting, air can play an important role in the ultimate finished product you enjoy.

After bottling, when wine is subsequently exposed to air, a couple of things happen: oxidation and evaporation. This effect, called aeration, reduces the presence of certain undesirable compounds, such as sulfites, making the wine more approachable, smoother and pleasantly aromatic. When you swirl the wine in your glass, you are aerating it.

Decanting– this is the act of pouring the wine in your bottle into some other, often fancier, container. I'm sure you have all been in a restaurant where a server (likely the sommelier) is pouring wine from the bottle into an elegant glass vessel, generally with a broader base and a thinner neck. Sometimes these can have names, like "duck" or "swan", and will resemble them!

While some air is good, too much can be a bad thing. If the cork in your bottle is flawed, too much air will enter the bottle over time and accelerate the oxidation process. If you hear the term "oxidized", that means the wine has developed a sherry-like color and matured too soon: white wines will start looking a little brown, and red wines will get brick (careful, certain red varietals can naturally have a bit of a brick hue) or even orange colored. At its worst, the chemical process turns the wine into vinegar.

COLOR, SMELL & TASTE

COLOR

How does wine get its color? It may come as a surprise, but the juice from grapes is generally clear. Most of the color in wine actually comes from the amount of skin contact during fermentation. The skins are where most of the pigments are found, and they will impart the wine's color, depending on the specific fermentation process. The skins are also where most of the wine's tannins come from.

So does that mean dark grapes produce red wine and light grapes produce white wine? For the most part, yes, but it is worth noting that one of the principal grapes used to produce sparkling wine, Pinot Noir, is a dark grape (Pinot Meunier is another).

And what about Rosé? Well, as you might imagine, it is just a question of how long the skins are left in the juice. When the winemaker has achieved the desired color, the juice is filtered off the skins and fermentation is completed like any other white wine.

There are other contributing factors to a wine's color (and Taste), such as the use of oak barrels to age the wine. Certain white wines such as Chardonnay are often, but not always, aged to one degree or another in oak, while other white wines will be aged in stainless steel tanks.

SMELL

Smell is so important to your overall enjoyment of wine. Unlike the tongue, which has a short list of tastes it can perceive, the nose is capable of identifying hundreds of different scents. Terms you will often hear are "aroma" or "nose". These refer to the smell of the wine in your glass. To truly appreciate the taste of a wine, follow your nose!

Wine aromas are often grouped into 3 categories: Primary; Secondary and Tertiary:

Primary aromas generally come from the grape variety. These tend to be identified as some form of fruit (black, red, tropical, etc) or flower. Sometimes primary aromas can also be described as spice-like or, herbal.

Secondary aromas tend to arise from the fermentation process, and are often characterized as earth-related (organic and inorganic), such as mushroom, forest floor, slate, wet gravel, etc.

Tertiary aromas come from aging and can be as varied as chocolate, leather, cigar box or vanilla. The most common influence here is the presence of oak.

TASTE

The human mouth has thousands of "taste buds", principally on the tongue, each containing up to 100 taste receptor cells. These buds can distinguish 5 established, basic tastes: Sweet; Sour (think Acidity, which is the term we will use); Salt; Bitter and "Umami" (think savory or meaty).

Taste buds alone do not fully account for how something tastes to us. Other factors include smell (the most important for wine as we just learned), texture and temperature.

Another taste sensation which comes into play with wine and, more specifically, food pairing is "hotness", sometimes referred to as piquancy, but for our purposes, let's just call it "spicy".

ALCOHOL:
Of course! But isn't it the same for all wine?

Alcohol content in wine can vary greatly, depending on climate and a variety of other factors. For the most part, the wines you will discover and enjoy have an alcohol content of somewhere between 10% and 15% ABV, or Alcohol By Volume. You can find this percentage right on the label.

White wines from cooler climate regions will have a low to medium-low alcohol content.
Red wines such as a California Zinfandel, a South African Pinotage or a Portuguese Touriga Nacional (originally used in Port) will be high in alcohol.

GLASSES

Having the proper kind of glass will help you fully appreciate your wine. While we won't get into the weeds on how & where the glass is made (although the Austrians really do make some of the best glasses...), there are a few helpful things to know.

Aromas contained in the vapors that come off the surface of the wine produce the majority of flavors that you actually perceive. The shape of the glass affects how these aromas are delivered to your nose:

> The wider the bowl, the more surface area exposed, which increases the alcohol evaporation. A wider opening helps collect the aromas. It also helps make red wine smoother. Note: a taller glass will help offset the impact of high tannins and alcohol. You can also drink fuller-bodied white wines such as Chardonnay from this style of glass.
>
> A glass with a slightly smaller bowl will be great for medium-to-full bodied red wines that have a more spicy character, such as Zinfandel, Syrah or Malbec. The spice note tends to get softened just a bit with this style of opening
>
> White wines as a rule are best served in smaller bowl glasses. This helps focus the fruit qualities, delivering more aromas (your nose is closer!) while helping to maintain a cooler temperature.
>
> For sparkling wine, keep it simple and serve in a tall, thin flute. The bubbles look great streaming up the glass!

PUTTING IT ALL TOGETHER

SERVING

There's a lot we could get into here about opening a wine bottle: corkscrews, sparkling wine tips & tricks, etiquette, etc. I will leave that for another time and place (maybe a Vlog?), but the one topic I do want to cover is Temperature. A few things to keep in mind:

Serving your wine at the proper temperature will allow you to fully enjoy what is in the glass. One temperature does not fit all, so to speak…

As a reference point, let's use "cellar temperature", which is generally considered to be 55-60 degrees fahrenheit.

Sparkling wines should be coldest (ice cold), then moving up the thermometer in order: light-bodied whites, full-bodied whites and rosés. Some rosés are better colder than others, but that can be a matter of personal taste. All of these should be below cellar temperature.

Light-bodied reds are good at cellar temperature, as well as some medium-bodied reds.

Medium to Full-bodied reds should be served at the top end of cellar temperature range, or slightly higher.

As a general rule, I find people serve their whites too cold and their reds too warm. If the wine is too cold, it will become closed-down and you won't be able to perceive all the aromas and flavors. If it is too warm, you will taste mostly alcohol and even bitterness.

TASTING:
Finally...!

This is the fun part, right? We don't open a bottle of wine to look at it; we open it to drink what's inside! Before taking that first sip, there are a few things you should do to fully appreciate what you are about to enjoy:

First of all, and this is something you *really* need to embrace, pour a modest amount of wine into the glass. As we learned earlier, the sense of smell is critical to our overall enjoyment. This is where those other supporting characters come into play: air and glass. If we don't have enough surface area of wine in the glass, and it doesn't have enough room to move, we won't be able to properly taste. This is particularly important when you are taking your first sips. Too often, people will pour too much into the glass. Don't be that person!!

Next, take the glass and swirl the wine to release its aromas. Swirling is where oxygen is our friend. From a science perspective, when we swirl we are aerating the wine and in the process releasing the multitude of aroma compounds. We are also coating the glass, which enhances what our nose is smelling.

You often hear the term "letting a wine breathe". Swirling the wine in your glass, or in the case of the whole bottle, decanting, is also allowing oxygen to begin to soften or round-out the tannins that may be present. Red wines can have higher levels of tannins when they are young. Oxygen helps the wine "open up".

Swirling is not a snobby thing to do, but it can sometimes look that way. It takes a little practice, but over time you will be able to do it precisely and quickly, with the glass in the air or flat on a table.

Start honing your skills with the glass on the table. What you want to do is grasp the glass at the bottom where the stem meets the base with two fingers. Most people use the thumb and forefinger; I prefer laying my right hand flat on the base so the stem is between my middle and forefinger. Then, all you do is draw tight, little circles on the table (I go counter-clockwise). Remember, it is best if there is just a small amount of wine in the glass. The trick is small…tight…circles.

Now, take a look at what is in the glass. Notice the color. Is it deeper or lighter? Deeper colored white wines probably have been aged in oak; lighter whites more likely in stainless steel. Deeper reds are probably younger and may have more intense tannins. Red wines can become paler as they age.

This is the moment when you will undoubtedly notice the tears or "legs" of wine running down the inside of the glass. This is the result of alcohol evaporation. Legs don't imply whether a wine is good or not. They do indicate the relative alcohol content. Higher alcohol wines such as Zinfandels will have pronounced, "denser" legs. Low alcohol wines, particularly whites, will have fewer, leaner, less defined legs.

After you swirl, put your nose into the glass and take a big sniff. Think about what you are smelling. Remember the different kinds of aromas we talked about earlier? Having the right kind of glass should not be underestimated. A proper wine glass should be of a size and shape that allows for a good swirl, has plenty of room for your nose and naturally concentrates the aromas.

Now…the moment we've been waiting for! Take a healthy sip and try to let it cover your palate before swallowing. This is where we bring all the components together to understand and appreciate what we are drinking. At this point, there is a lot going on in your mouth. To help you organize all the inputs, there are a few key terms you should learn and keep in mind every time you taste:

BODY

This is a way to describe the overall intensity of the wine, from light to rich, or "light-bodied" to "full-bodied". Body can also be described as "texture". Does the wine fill or coat your mouth with flavor, or is it more subtle? What you perceive the wine's body to be will be influenced by the following components:

Acidity – wines with higher acidity taste lighter-bodied, those with lower acidity taste fuller-bodied. High acidity wines like Sauvignon Blanc will often have a zesty, bright feeling in the mouth. If the wine's acidity level is too low, the wine can seem flat or dull ("flabby" is a wine term you may hear).

Alcohol – the higher the alcohol, the more full-bodied it will seem. That warming sensation in your throat is the alcohol.

Sweetness – sweetness will increase the body in wine. As we now know, sweetness comes from what is called residual sugar.

Tannin – increases the body in wine. Red wines taste more full-bodied because they have tannins; white wines lack tannins so they taste lighter-bodied. Science alert: Tannins are polyphenols and have antioxidant properties. Tannin comes from the skins and seeds of grapes. It also comes from oak aging. Tannins will give you that astringent or drying sensation in your mouth.

FINISH

This refers to the taste or flavors that you perceive at the end. In essence, this is the wine's aftertaste. Are they similar to what you noticed at the beginning, or has it changed?

LENGTH

Length is simply a measure of the amount of time you continue to sense the taste and aroma of the wine after swallowing. Does it stay with you, or does it quickly and cleanly dissipate?

VALUE:
What does QPR mean??

Simply stated, QPR stands for Quality Price Ratio. Nothing too scientific, just a concept that tries to highlight relative value in a wine. As you become more experienced, with more of those "data points" on your palate, you will be able to draw comparisons about price vs quality. Our objective is always to find wines that "drink better than their price".

Said another way, if the $15 bottle you were pouring demonstrated qualities you would typically expect to find in wines $20 or more (and you would be willing to pay more for it), you'd say that $15 bottle had a high QPR. In non-wine terms, you'd say the wine was punching above its weight..

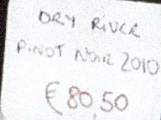

FOOD & WINE:
Where to begin??

This is such a big topic, I am more or less going to punt on this one. It deserves more time and space than I can give it here, and frankly goes a little beyond my objectives for this simple publication.

However...because food and wine are natural partners, and most of the time you will be enjoying wine with food, a few pointers are in order. If you want to do a deeper dive on food & wine in a very user-friendly way, I recommend you look up Madeline Puckette and her amazing wine education site **"Wine Folly"**. She combines an incredible depth of wine knowledge with one-of-a-kind graphics of her own creation to make everything easy to understand. She's also very funny.

Here are some food & wine basics Madeline and others teach...

> Think about wine as an ingredient. There are two fundamental pairing methodologies for food & wine: Congruent and Contrasting. The objective of either one is to create "balance".
>
> Congruent pairing is more often associated with Western dishes: think Barbeque with Zinfandel, Thanksgiving dinner with Pinot Noir, etc.
>
> Contrasting pairing can be associated with more Eastern cuisines: think Asian food and an off-dry Riesling, or Curry flavored dishes and Gruner Veltliner (Austria's #1 varietal, also makes a great pairing with oysters).

Some other great-to-remember Food & Wine pro tips:

The wine should be more acidic than the food

The wine should have the same "intensity" as the food

Fats and oils balance high-tannin wines (think steak with Cabernet Sauvignon, Tempranillo from Spain, an Italian Barolo or a Portugese red made with Touriga Nacional)

Generally, whites, rosés and sparkling wines create contrasting pairings; red wines generally create congruent pairings.

Bottom line, this is "learn as you go". Have fun and, over time, you will find yourself making some good choices and taking your Wine Experience to a whole new level.

CHEERS!

ABOUT THE BOOK

MICHAEL MONTE (THE WINE DOCTOR)
Author

Michael Monte is a wine expert, educator and author of the popular wine website and blog "The Wine Doctor" (*www.thewinemd.com*). While not a real doctor, his tasting experience always results in the right wine prescription! Michael wanted to create a non-threatening, easy-to-read way to learn about wine. That vision has culminated in his new book, Wine Made Easy: Wine 101 for Everyone. As he says in the introductory page of his website: "So let's get started- the Doctor is in!"

MARY TJOTJOS
Graphic Designer

Mary Tjotjos is an artist and graphic designer. In 2019 she graduated from the DAAP (Design, Art, Architecture and Planning) program at the University of Cincinnati with an award for the *Most Outstanding Art Student in the Class of 2019*. Since then, she has worked for a global magazine and designed and released 4 publications. Michael and Mary first partnered up to create the Wine Doctor logo. Now, they have joined forces again to create this beautiful, easy-to-read book for wine lovers of all levels.

www.ingramcontent.com/pod-product-compliance
Lightning Source LLC
Chambersburg PA
CBHW061750290426
44108CB00028B/2941